THREE REGAL MARCHES FOR ORGAN
VOLUME 2

Table of Contents

Grimoaldo Macchia

Dedicated to Christopher Herrick, concert organist

Trumpet Tune for a Festive Day

Sw. Principals 8', 4', 2'
Gt. Solo Trumpet
Ch. Principals 8', 4'
Ped. Foundations 16', 8'

Grimoaldo Macchia

Maestoso ♩ = ca. 72

Gt. Trumpet or Cornet
f a tempo
Sw.
rit.
a tempo
poco rit.
D.C. al Coda

Coda
19
Gt. +4'
f
Sw.
Ped. +Reeds
22
24
poco rit.
Gt. -4'
f
a tempo
Ch.
mf
Ped. -Reeds
mf
27

29
tr
31
33
Full Organ
poco rit.
a tempo
Ped. +Reeds
ff
35
rit.
Ped. +Bombarde

Dedicated to Bernadette Kumschick

Trompette for Bernadette

Sw. Principals 8', 4'
Gt. Full Organ
Ch. Solo Trumpet
Ped. Foundations 16', 8'

Grimoaldo Macchia

Moderato ♩= ca. 116

17
Ch.
f
Sw.
mf
mf
22
26
30

34
38
rit.
43
Ch.
f
a tempo
Sw.
mf
mf
47

51
Gt.
ff
f
55
59
Ch. (2nd time: Fl. 8', 2', 1⅓')
f
Sw.
mf
mf
63

67
72
77
1
2
82
rit.
Gt.
fff
a tempo

87
92
Ch. Solo Trumpet
ff
Sw.
f
97
rit.
a tempo
+Gt. to Ped.
102
allargando
Tutti
fff

For Oliver and Melanie

Royal Trumpet Tune

Sw. Foundations 8', 4', Mix. IV
Gt. Foundations 8', 4'
Ch. Solo Trumpet
Ped. Foundations 16', 8', Reed 16'

Grimoaldo Macchia

Festoso ♩ = 72

9
Sw.
f
12
15
18

21
Ch.
f
Gt.
23
25
27
tr
Ch. Add to or change Solo
f
3

29
(staccato)
mf
tr
31
33
tr
35
rit.

Ch. Solo Trumpet
37
f
Gt.
39
41
43
rit.